The Poet's Notebook

Inspiration, Techniques, and Advice on Craft

Created by David Stanford Burr

RUNNING PRESS

PHILADELPHIA · LONDON

ISBN 0-7624-0824-3

Designed by Ellen Lohse
Edited by Jason Rekulak

This book may be ordered by mail from the publisher.
Please include $2.50 for postage and handling.
But try your bookstore first!

Running Press Book Publishers
125 South Twenty-second Street
Philadelphia, Pennsylvania 19103-4399

Visit us on the web!
www.runningpress.com

A NOTE TO THE POET

Fellow poet, this is *your* notebook: Use it well and be well rewarded! Carry it wherever you go, and write in it whenever you can: on the train or bus, in the library, café, or museum, over breakfast or dinner. Take the time to develop your poetic voice. Use these pages to preserve your observations and impressions while people-watching. Capture that fleeting image you tell yourself you *will* remember—that idea, that rhyme, that killer line.

This notebook will aid you in recording the best poem you can write—the best stanzas and lines, the best words and titles. And if you're "blocked," use these pages to brainstorm ideas, write about why you cannot write, jot down your dreams, or attempt the suggested exercises throughout this book. If you'd like to try writing in a form—like a sonnet, villanelle, sestina, pantoum, or haiku—some guidelines are listed in the appendix, along with celebrated examples to read—out loud.

Also featured throughout this notebook are observations and advice from thirty-seven different poets (who can collectively claim four Nobel and twenty-six Pulitzer Prizes for poetry). Read their words, tackle the practice exercises and traditional forms, but start writing *right now*—off the top of your head and without censorship. This will often jump-start a poem, or provide the kernel of a poem that you'll write later. And when you've filled the pages of this notebook, begin another—but don't forget to go back and look over what you've written. You'll be surprised at how old material can, upon reflection, provide fresh grist for your poetry mill, and trigger the finished poems you wouldn't have written otherwise.

Start your imagination's engines!

—David Stanford Burr

I save all my notebooks, and from time to time when I don't
know what I'm going to write, I read them over and find the first line of
a poem which I started but couldn't finish and sometimes I'm able to finish it.
Nothing you write is ever lost to you. At some other
level your mind is working on it.

Notebooks

—Erica Jong (b. 1942)

There is that rare poem spun whole from an image
buried in the yellowing pages of a haphazard
notebook, and I call such a poem a gift.
_____

—Yusef Komunyakaa (b. 1947)

I think it's awfully dangerous to give general advice.
I think the best one can do for a young poet is to criticize in
detail a particular poem of his. Argue it with him if necessary; give
him your opinion, and if there are any generalizations
to be made, let him do them himself.

—T. S. Eliot (1888–1965)

OLD PHOTO ALBUMS CAN YIELD A TREASURE TROVE OF INSPIRATION. WRITE A POEM ABOUT THE MINUTES LEADING UP TO A GROUP SNAPSHOT. OR STUDY A PHOTOGRAPH OF YOURSELF AS A CHILD AND JOT DOWN AS MUCH AS YOU CAN RECALL OF THAT TIME IN PRECISE DETAIL AND SPECIFIC IMAGES.

Photo Moments

Around the Corner

[The young poet] should stay the hell out of writing classes and find out what's happening around the corner. And bad luck for the young poet would be a rich father, an early marriage, an early success or the ability to do anything very well.

—Charles Bukowski (1920–1994)

I wish our clever young poets would remember my
homely definitions of prose and poetry; that is,
prose—words in their best order;
poetry—the best words in their best order.

Poetry

—*Samuel Taylor Coleridge (1772—1834)*

Is encouragement what the poet needs?
Open question. Maybe he needs discouragement.
In fact, quite a few of them need more discouragement,
the most discouragement possible.

Question —Robert Fitzgerald (1910—1985)

If I had to "teach poetry," which thank God, I don't, I would
concentrate on prosody, rhetoric . . . and learning poems by heart.
I may be quite wrong, but I don't see what can
be learned except purely technical things. *Concentrate*

—W. H. Auden (1907–1973)

Prosody IS THE STUDY OF THE FORMAL STRUCTURE OF VERSE, SUCH AS SOUND-PATTERNING (INCLUDING RHYME), METER, AND STANZA.

Very few people at any one time ever write poetry that is any good.
But surely all of them will read it and teach it with greater sympathy
and understanding for having tried to write some. *Write*

———

—W. D. Snodgrass (b. 1926)

The Sincerest Form of Flattery

CLOSELY READ THE WORK OF YOUR FAVORITE POET, THEN WRITE A POEM IN HIS OR HER STYLE. TRY TO CAST THEIR APPROACH ON SUBJECT MATTER THAT INTERESTS YOU MOST.

I'm sure that writing isn't a craft, that is, something for which you learn the skills and go on turning out. It must come from some deep impulse, deep inspiration. That can't be taught, it can't be what you use in teaching. *Inspiration*

—*Robert Lowell* (1917–1977)

You run into people who want to write poetry who don't want
to read anything in the tradition. That's like wanting to be a builder
but not finding out what different kinds of wood you use.

Tradition ————

—*Gary Snyder (b. 1930)*

I didn't really get a feeling for the poetry of the past until I had discovered
modern poetry. Then I began to see how nineteenth-century poetry
wasn't just something lifeless in an ancient museum but must
have grown out of the lives of the people who wrote it. *Discover*

—*John Ashberry (b. 1927)*

Everything I have written is the result of reading or of interest in people,
I'm sure of that. I had no ambition to be a writer.

Ambition

—Marianne Moore (1887–1972)

A word on Academies; poetry has been attacked by an
ignorant & frightened bunch of bores who don't understand
how it's made, & the trouble with these creeps is they wouldn't
know Poetry if it came up and buggered them in broad daylight.

Academies ————————

—*Allen Ginsberg (1926–1997)*

Single Poet Seeking Inspiration

TURN TO THE PERSONAL ADS IN YOUR LOCAL NEWSPAPER AND WRITE ABOUT THAT TRAMPY "SINGLE 21 YO FEMALE ISO WEALTHY, OLDER GENTLEMAN." BETTER YET, WRITE YOUR OWN PERSONAL AD IN THE FORM OF A POEM.

Words

I fell in love—that is the only expression I can think of—at once, and am still at the mercy of words, though sometimes now, knowing a little of their behavior very well, I think I can influence them slightly and have learned to beat them now and then, which they appear to enjoy.

—*Dylan Thomas (1914–1953)*

The idea for a poem comes in moments of personal excitement. I sometimes jot down a few prose lines in a notebook, leaving them purposely vague. Then begins the process *Personal* of gradually giving the poem rhythmical form. *Excitement*——Rhythm produces a faint hypnosis.

—W. B. Yeats (1865–1939)

The first discipline is the realization that there *is*
a discipline—that all art begins and ends with discipline,
that any art is first and foremost a craft.

Discipline

—*Archibald MacLeish (1892–1982)*

One only arrives at a useful precision in spontaneous art
if there's been a lot of discipline in one's life earlier. Dr. Johnson said,
"what is written without effort is in general read without pleasure."

Effort

—*Richard Wilbur (b. 1921)*

So if you are using rhyme…
when you're heading towards those last couple of syllables, and
you're desperate, and you don't know what it's going to be…[rhyme]
can alter meaning…and what you then do is you have to
follow what the subterranean thing that has suddenly *Alter*
emerged dominates in your direction.

Meaning

—*Derek Walcott (b. 1930)*

Rhyme AN ECHO OF SOUNDS THAT RESONATE IN AN AURAL PATTERN, HAS SEVERAL DIFFERENT EXPRESSIONS: PERFECT, IMPERFECT, MASCULINE, FEMININE, CONSONANTAL, ASSONANTAL, SLANT, AND DISSONANT. RHYME CAN FALL AT THE END OF THE LINE OR CREATE AN INTERNAL WEB OF LIKE SOUNDS.

The poet who writes "free" verse is like Robinson Crusoe on his desert island: he must do all his cooking, laundry, and darning for himself. In a few exceptional cases, this manly independence produces something original and impressive, but more often the result is *Independence* squalor—dirty sheets on the unmade bed and empty bottles on the unswept floor.

—W. H. Auden (1907–1973)

Free Verse IS NOT COMPOSED IN TRADITIONAL METRICAL FORM AND/OR DOES NOT FOLLOW FIXED PLACEMENT ON THE PAGE. MUCH CONTEMPORARY VERSE IS FREE VERSE, WHERE ORGANIC REQUIREMENTS DICTATE THE POEM'S DEVELOPMENT.

I like Eliot's sentence:
"No verse is *libre* for the man who wants to do a good job."
I think the best free verse comes from an
attempt to get back to quantitative meter
[patterns of long and short vowel length].

———————

—*Ezra Pound (1885–1972)*

Go Against Your Style:

If you write in free verse, switch to metrics. If you write long lines, shorten them. If you write a poem as a block of type, break it up into stanzas. Vary your routine and see what develops.

Actually, free verse is not a term that I myself care much for....
What you are talking about is that you are not writing

Organic a rhyming or a regular verse,
but more of an open, organic form. *Form*

————————

—James Dickey (1923–1997)

Stop

Any work of art makes one very simple demand on anyone who genuinely wants to get in touch with it. And that is to stop. You've got to stop what you're doing, what you're thinking, and what you're expecting and just be there for the poem for however long it takes.

—W. S. Merwin (b. 1927)

An English poet, Philip Larkin, said that
poetry doesn't start with an idea; it starts with a poem....
Open to You have to be open to mystery.
If you are open to it, mystery will come.
If you're not, why should it, actually? *Mystery*

—Lucille Clifton (b. 1936)

Random Inspiration:

SELECT FIFTEEN RANDOM VERBS, NOUNS, AND ADJECTIVES FROM THE DICTIONARY AND SEE IF THE COMBINED LIST SUGGESTS A THEME. MOST PEOPLE ONLY USE THE SAME EIGHT THOUSAND WORDS IN EVERYDAY CONVERSATION, BUT YOU HAVE TENS OF THOUSANDS MORE AT YOUR DISPOSAL.

Those moments before a poem comes,
when the heightened awareness comes over you, and you
realize a poem is buried there somewhere, you prepare yourself.
I run around, you know, kind of skipping
around the house, marvelous elation.
It's as though I could fly.

Elation

—*Anne Sexton (1928—1974)*

Decisions At that moment I made one of the most important decisions of life. I dropped my hoe and ran into the house and started to write this poem ["End of Summer"]. It began as a celebration of wild geese. Eventually the geese flew out of the poem, but I like to think they left behind the sound of their beating wings.

—Stanley Kunitz (b. 1905)

It takes patience and when you find the well,
or when the well finds you—and sometimes that's the
case—it can be very frightening because the well pulls you down
into yourself in a way that threatens your ability to communicate.

Patience

—Rita Dove (b. 1952)

Automatic While there is nothing automatic about the poem, nevertheless it has an automatic aspect in the sense that it is what I wanted it to be without knowing before it was written what I wanted it to be, even though I knew before it was written what I wanted to do.

———————

—*Wallace Stevens (1879–1955)*

Get
Political:

Take on the personality of a politician in the news and write a rant in his voice, or have her deliver a public apology. Describe the rage an ultraright Christian Conservative feels when listening to a radical liberal Democrat . . . or vice versa.

At any given time, I have two things on my mind: a theme
that interests me and a problem of verbal form, meter, diction, etc,
The theme looks for the right form: the form looks for the right theme.
When the two come together, I am able to start writing.

Theme

—W. H. Auden (1907–1973)

The writing's easy, it's the living that is sometimes difficult.

—*Charles Bukowski* (1920–1994)

Living

A poem always has elements of accident about it, which can be made the subject of inquest afterwards, but there is always a risk in conducting your own inquest: you might begin to believe the coroner in yourself rather than put your trust in the man in you who is capable of the accident.

Risk

—Seamus Heaney (b. 1939)

A writer is unfair to himself when he's
not willing to be hard on himself.

Willing

—*Marianne Moore (1887–1972)*

I went for years not finishing anything.
Because, of course, when you finish something you can be judged....
I had poems which were rewritten so many times I suspect
it was just a way of avoiding sending them out.

————————

—Erica Jong (b. 1942)

Finish

I would find a crumpled yellow ball of paper in *Slight*
the wastebasket, in the morning, and open it to see what *Change*
the hell I'd been up to; and occasionally it was something that
needed only a very slight change to be brought off,
which I'd missed the day before.

—Conrad Aiken (1889–1973)

Desk top Inspiration:

SOMETIMES POETRY CAN BE WAITING RIGHT IN FRONT OF YOU. DEVISE A "LIST POEM" DESCRIBING THE ITEMS ON YOUR DESK; HAVE THE SELECTION OF ITEMS REVEAL SOMETHING INTERESTING ABOUT THEIR OWNER.

Whatever was there is replaceable.
In fact, often in revising I will remove the idea that was the original stimulus.
I think I am more interested in the movement among ideas than in the ideas themselves,
the way one goes from one point to another rather than the destination or the origin.

—*John Ashberry* (b. 1927)

Movement

I keep the successive drafts of a poem to myself,
because I conceive the poetic process as quite a private matter between
the poet, his hand, and the blazing white island of paper which
he is trying to populate or eliminate. *Private*
—————
—James Dickey (1923–1997)

I don't actually revise, or it's very seldom that I revise.
What I do is write so leisurely that all the revisions occur in thought
or in the margins of the page. It can make for a page which is as dense, graphically,
as some men's-room walls. Which is not to say that a poem is like going to the men's room.

Revise

—*Richard Wilbur (b. 1921)*

Experience I work very slowly and doggedly.
Eight or nine years doesn't surprise me at all; I think I've got one that took me
about fifteen. I mean I carried the experience around that long, trying it
in this poem, that poem, finally getting one that I thought worked.

—W. D. Snodgrass (b. 1926)

My own revisions are usually the result of impatience with unkempt diction
and lapses in logic, together with an awareness that for
most defects, to delete is the instantaneous cure.

———————

—*Marianne Moore* (1887–1972)

Confession seems to me to be [related to] sin....
But I do not think that writing apparently personal poetry, which is what
people seem to be calling confessional poetry, has
to do with wrongdoing and asking for forgiveness. *Personal*

—*Sharon Olds (b. 1942)*

Start a Dialogue:

CONSTRUCT AN IMAGINARY CONVERSATION BETWEEN YOU AND SOMEONE YOU CARED FOR WHO IS DEAD OR FAR AWAY. WHAT WOULD YOU TELL THEM IF YOU HAD THE CHANCE? WHAT WOULD YOU WANT THEM TO SAY—OR NOT SAY—TO YOU?

Choice

I haven't ever intended to put myself directly
into the poems, not in any of the poems I've written. I've always felt it
was an author's privilege to leave himself out if he chose—and I chose,
contrary to the choice of certain friends and contemporaries.

————

—*Donald Justice (b. 1925)*

Facts   In a poem dealing with my personal experience
I do much better simply saying exactly what happened.
That will usually carry more emotional depth. When I'm trying to get
to what I really feel about something, I usually do better just sticking to the facts.

———————

—*W. D. Snodgrass (b. 1926)*

Sometimes my doctors tell me that I understand something
in a poem that I haven't integrated into my life.
In fact, I may be concealing it from myself, *Understand*
while revealing it to the readers.

—*Anne Sexton (1928–1974)*

Analyze This:

WRITE AN *HONEST* CONFESSION, SHARE A
DARK SECRET, AUTHOR YOUR CREDO OF
PERSONAL TRUTHS, ADDRESS A POEM TO
YOURSELF FROM YOURSELF. COMPLETE A
TWENTY-LINE POEM WHERE THE BEGINNING
OF EACH LINE IS "GIVE ME...," THEN ONE
THAT BEGINS "I WILL NOT..."

We all know that the power of a great poem
is not that we felt that person expressed himself well.
We don't think that. What we think is "How deeply *I* am touched."
That's our level of response. And so a great poet does not
express his or her self; he expresses *all* of our selves.

Response

—*Gary Snyder (b. 1930)*

You don't choose a story, it chooses you. You get together with that story somehow; you're stuck with it. There certainly is some reason it attracted you, *Reason* and you're writing it trying to find out that reason.

———

—*Robert Penn Warren (1905–1989)*

There must not be any preconceived notion or *design* for what the poem *ought* to be....
I'm not interested in writing sonnets, sestinas or anything...only poems.
If the poem has got to be a sonnet (unlikely tho) or whatever,
it'll certainly let me know.

Design

——————

—*Amiri Baraka (b. 1934)*

The wildest poem has to have a firm basis in common sense, and this, I think, is the advantage of formal verse. Aside from the obvious corrective advantages, formal verse frees one from the fetters of one's ego.

Formal Verse

—W. H. Auden (1907–1973)

Absolutely

If by traditional forms we mean meters, stanzas, rhymes, that kind of thing, I don't think any of those has any meaning in itself or is absolutely essential to poetry.

Essential

———————

—*Richard Wilbur (b. 1921)*

True to Form:

USING THE FORMS AND POEMS SECTION AT THE BACK OF THIS BOOK, WRITE A HAIKU DESCRIBING A FALLING LEAF, A VILLANELLE RELIVING AN OLD LOVE AFFAIR, OR A SESTINA PRESENTING A RÉSUMÉ OF YOUR STRENGTHS AND FAILINGS AS A HUMAN BEING.

Heart of the Matter

Images are probably the most important part of the poem.
First of all you want to tell a story, but images are what
are going to shore it up and get to the heart of the matter.

—Anne Sexton (1928–1974)

An Image IS A PICTURE OR OTHER SENSUAL DESCRIPTION THAT HAS AN IMMEDIATE EMOTIONAL AND INTELLECTUAL EFFECT. IN SHAKESPEARE'S *OTHELLO*, *JEALOUSY* IS DEFINED IN A METAPHOR AS "THE GREEN-EY'D MONSTER," WHICH, TODAY HAS BECOME A CLICHÉ, DUE UNFORTUNATELY TO ITS SINGULAR EVOCATION DONE TO DEATH BY CENTURIES OF REPETITION.

The distinguishing mark of the poet, that aptitude which more than
any other skill of the mind makes him a poet, is metaphor, according to Aristotle.
Now metaphor is literally a bearing-across, or a bringing-together of things by means of words.

———————

Distinguishing Mark —Delmore Schwartz (1913–1966)

A Metaphor IS A FIGURE OF SPEECH THAT DECLARES TWO OR MORE DISSIMILAR ELEMENTS ARE EQUIVALENT. SHAKESPEARE'S *ROMEO AND JULIET:* "IT IS THE EAST, AND JULIET IS THE SUN."

Like a piece of ice on a hot stove the poem
must ride on its own melting.
—————————

The Poem

—Robert Frost (1874–1963)

A Simile

INDIRECTLY COMPARES TWO OR MORE DISSIMILAR ELEMENTS USING *LIKE* OR *AS*. ROBERT BURNS'S (1759–1796) POEM, "A RED, RED ROSE" BEGINS WITH THE LINE, "O MY LUVE'S LIKE A RED, RED ROSE," WHICH CONTAINS A SIMILE.

I find it difficult to understand the mystique of line lengths obeying the breath, by rules.
I just don't understand that, though some people seem to. *Obeying*
I should think, in that case, that if the poet lived *the*
long enough and developed emphysema,
his lines would become shorter, more *Breath*
ragged, more desperate. Fewer.
——————

—*Donald Justice (b. 1925)*

Line Length CAN BE METRICALLY DETERMINED BY THE NUMBER OF SYLLABLES; NUMBER OF ACCENTS; AND NUMBER OF SYLLABLES AND ACCENTS IN A LINE, AND, IN QUANTITATIVE METER, BY THE LENGTH OF SYLLABLES. IN FREE VERSE, LINEATION DEPENDS ON THE UNIQUE, INTERNAL LOGIC OF THE POEM.

I became almost intoxicated by the idea of the line break.
It seemed as if I were writing just to get to this point, this decision.
But, although the line break is very important to me, I don't really
Line understand how I know when it is supposed to happen. *Break*

—*John Ashberry (b. 1927)*

The Poet's

LINE BREAK DECISIONS ARE CRUCIAL. *END-STOPPED* LINES ARE COMPLETE IN METER AND SENSE AND OFTEN HAVE PUNCTUATION AT THEIR END. AN *ENJAMBED* LINE FORCES THE READER TO COMPLETE THE SENSE OF A LINE BY CONTINUING TO THE FOLLOWING LINE.

The accuracy of the vernacular! That's the kind of thing
I am interested in, am always taking down
little local expressions and accents. *Vernacular*

———————

—*Marianne Moore (1887—1972)*

Try a Persona Poem:

ADOPT THE VOICE AND CHARACTERISTICS OF SOMEONE OF A DIFFERENT GENDER, RACE, NATIONALITY, OR AGE, OR SOMEONE WITH A HANDICAP. DEVELOP THEIR PERSONALITIES AND VOICES. FIND OUT WHAT THEY HAVE TO SAY.

I used to listen to [Charlie] Parker's endless variations on
"I Got Rhythm" and all the various times in which he'd play it,
all the tempi, up, down, you name it. What fascinated me was

Silences that he'd write silences as actively as sounds,
which of course they were. Just so in poetry.

———————

—*Robert Creeley (b. 1926)*

I never write except with a writing board. I've never had a table in my life.
And I use all sorts of things. Write on the sole of my shoe.

Writing Board —Robert Frost (1874–1963)

I've never had a schedule. I go simply by impulse, whim.
What I do try to do is to keep my life uncluttered when I'm not teaching,
and therefore be able to harden to the first whisper of any idea.

Schedule

—Richard Wilbur (b. 1921)

Change Your Routine: If you usually write in the mornings, try writing at night, or vice versa. If you've always worked at home, try writing in a coffee shop or a commuter train or a bench in the local shopping mall. New surroundings can often yield unexpected results.

I feel blocked much less often, though it still happens.
It's important to try to write when you are in the wrong mood
or the weather is wrong. Even if you don't succeed you'll be
developing a muscle that may do it later on. *Blocked*

—John Ashberry (b. 1927)

When I had a minute or two, I'd throw a poem into the typewriter
and try to work out a line or get a transition from one stanza to the next.
But the business world gives you almost no time to do anything but business.
You are selling your soul to the devil all day and trying to buy it back at night.

Business

———

—James Dickey (1923–1997)

I suspect that everybody has dry periods. One advantage of getting older is that you have been through it before and before and before: though it doesn't do very *much* good, you can tell yourself that you will come out of it, that you will write again, and therefore you can stay somewhat this side of despair.

Dry Periods

—*Richard Wilbur (b. 1921)*

With some of the later poems I've written out prose versions,
then cut the prose down and abbreviated it....
Prose And it's a nice technical problem:
how can you keep phrases and get them into meter?

——————

—*Robert Lowell (1917—1977)*

So Prosaic Well, this [see preceding quotation] is really the darndest way of writing a poem that I ever heard of, and I don't think it's any wonder that sometimes his things sound so—so prosaic.

—*Conrad Aiken (1889–1973)*

Poetry is honored by much generosity and much prestige. Unfortunately, these are provided after the poet has established himself—and not always then—but during the first and perhaps most difficult years of being a poet, the best thing a poet can do is get some other job to support his effort to be a poet. *Established*

—*Delmore Schwartz (1913–1966)*

I thought I should do something to celebrate, have a glass of wine
or something. But all I could find in that house, a friend's, were
some cookies from America, some awful chocolate cookies—
Oreos, I think—so I ended up eating two of those.
And that's how I celebrated winning
the Pulitzer Prize.

Celebrate

—*Elizabeth Bishop (1911–1979)*

Your Worst Nightmare:

Imagine that your mother or father has found this notebook, and read all of its contents. Then write from their point of view, describing their reaction to your poetry. Are they proud? Angry? Indifferent? *Be honest.*

Unlikely To have written one good poem—good used seriously—is an unlikely and marvelous thing that only a couple hundred writers of English, at the most, have done—it's like sitting out in the yard in the evening and having a meteorite fall in one's lap. *and Marvelous*

—Randall Jarrell (1914–1965)

Perfectly There's nothing so wonderful as having constructed something perfectly arbitrary, without any help from anybody else, out of pure delight and self-delight, and then to find that it turns out to be useful to a few others. *Arbitrary*

—*Richard Wilbur (b. 1921)*

Forms and Poems

SONNET

Begun in Italy eight hundred years ago, this verse form consists of an octave (eight-line stanza) followed by a sestet (six-line stanza). It is customarily written in iambic pentameter, the most common meter in English poetry—which is a meter of five feet, each containing a short (unaccented) then a long (accented) syllable, for a line length of ten syllables.

The sonnet usually has a single thought or emotion as its theme. The argument of the poem is laid out in the first half of the octave, developed in the second, then after a "turn" of thought, the first tercet (three-line stanza) of the sestet reflects on the octave and the final tercet draws the poem to a logical, forceful close. The previous sentence describes the most widely used sonnet form, the Petrarchan, which has a rhyme scheme of *abbaabba*, *cdecde*. The two main contenders, Spenserian (*ababbcbccdcdee*) and Shakespearean (*abab, cdcd, efef, gg*), end with a rhymed couplet. Here is a Shakespearean sonnet by its namesake, William Shakespeare (1564–1616):

Sonnet 18

Shall I compare thee to a summer's day?
Thou art more lovely and more temperate:
Rough winds do shake the darling buds of May,
And summer's lease hath all too short a date;
Sometime too hot the eye of heaven shines,
And often is his gold complexion dimm'd,
And every fair from fair sometime declines,
By chance or nature's changing course untrimm'd:
But thy eternal summer shall not fade,
Nor lose possession of that fair thou ow'st,
Nor shall Death brag thou wand'rest in his shade,
When in eternal lines to time thou grow'st,
  So long as men can breathe or eyes can see,
  So long lives this, and this gives life to thee.

VILLANELLE

This Italian verse form was standardized in seventeenth-century France and is contains five tercets, rhymed *aba*, and a concluding quatrain (four-line stanza), rhymed *abaa*, for a total of nineteen lines. The lines may be any length but are generally written in iambic pentameter (see *Sonnet*). Only two rhymes are used and the first and third lines of the initial tercet repeat alternately as the third line of each following tercet, and both lines repeat as the last two lines of the concluding quatrain. The rhyme and refrain scheme is A^1bA^2, abA^1, abA^2, abA^1, abA^2, abA^1A^2. Here is Ernest Dowson's (1867–1900) offering:

Villanelle of his lady's treasures

I took her dainty eyes, as well
    As silken tendrils of her hair:
And so I made a Villanelle!

I took her voice, a silver bell,
    As clear as song, as soft as prayer;
I took her dainty eyes as well.

It may be, said I, who can tell,
    These things shall be my less despair?
And so I made a Villanelle!

I took her whiteness virginal
    And from her cheek two roses rare:
I took her dainty eyes as well.

I said: "It may be possible
    Her image from my heart to tear!"
And so I made a Villanelle.

I stole her laugh, most musical:
    I wrought it in with artful care;
I took her dainty eyes as well;
And so I made a Villanelle.

SESTINA

This verse form, invented by the twelfth-century Provençal troubadour Daniel Arnaut, spread to Italy, Spain, and Portugal, then to France. The English version is a syllabic form of six sestets and a concluding triplet, called an envoy, for a total of thirty-nine lines. Instead of end rhyme the six end-words of the first sestet recur in a fixed pattern for the next five sestets, with the envoy using all six end-words.

It may sound confusing, but there is a pattern: Using numbers to indicate the end-words, the pattern is 123456, 615243, 364125, 532614, 451362, 246531, with the envoy ending in 531 or 135. The end-words 2, 4, and, 6 are also used in the middle of the envoy's lines, so each line contains two of the end-words.

Here is an example from Algernon Charles Swinburne (1873–1909), who departs from the usual end-word pattern but increases the difficulty by rhyming the initial sestet *ababab*:

Sestina

I saw my soul at rest upon a day
As a bird sleeping in the nest of night,
Among soft leaves that give the starlight way
To touch its wings but not its eyes with light;
So that it knew as one in visions may,
And knew not as men waking, of delight.

This was the measure of my soul's delight;
It had no power of joy to fly by day,
Nor part in the large lordship of the light;
But in a secret moon-beholden way
Had all its will of dreams and pleasant night,
And all the love and life that sleepers may.

But such life's triumph as men waking may
It might not have to feed its faint delight
Between the stars by night and sun by day,
Shut up with green leaves and a little light;
Because its way was a lost star's way,
A world's not wholly known of day or night.

All loves and dreams and sounds and gleams of night
Made it all music that such minstrels may,
And all they had they gave it of delight;
But in the full face of the fire of day
What place shall be for any starry light,
What part of heaven in all the wide sun's way?

Yet the soul woke not, sleeping by the way,
Watched as a nursling of the large eyed night,
And sought no strength nor knowledge of the day,
Nor closer touch conclusive of delight,
Nor mightier joy nor truer than dreamers may,
Nor more of song than they, nor more of light.

For who sleeps once and sees the secret light
Whereby sleep shows the soul a fairer way
Between the rise and rest of day and night,
Shall care no more to fare as all men may,
But be his place of pain or of delight,
There shall he dwell, beholding night as day.

Song, have thy day and take thy fill of light
Before the night be fallen across the way;
Sing while he may, man hath no long delight.

PANTOUM

This Malay verse form, popular in France and England in the nineteenth century, is a poem of varying length comprised of quatrains in a fixed *abab* rhyme scheme where the second and fourth line of each stanza repeats as the first and third of the next stanza, and so on. The concluding quatrain, however, must have its second and fourth lines repeat the third and first lines of the initial stanza. The rhyme and refrain scheme (for a four-stanza pantoum) is $A^1B^1A^2B^2$, $B^1C^1B^2C^2$, $C^1D^1C^2D^2$, $D^1A^2D^2A^1$. The form is interesting in that it begins and concludes with the same line, and the intervening lines of argument force a different interpretation of the line when encountered the second time. The lines need not follow a prescribed length or meter but usually have a fixed number of syllables and pattern of accents. Though rarely used by English-writing poets, this form can yield surprising and humorous results, as Henry Austin Dobson (1840–1921) demonstrates. Note how Dobson departs from the "rule" in the last quatrain:

In Town

'The blue fly sung in the pane.'—Tennyson.

Toiling in Town now is 'horrid,'
(There is that woman again!)—
June in the zenith is torrid,
Thought gets dry in the brain.

There is that woman again:
'Strawberries! fourpence a pottle!'
Thought gets dry in the brain;
Ink gets dry in the bottle.

'Strawberries! fourpence a pottle!'
Oh for the green of a lane!—

Ink gets dry in the bottle;
'Buzz' goes a fly in the pane!

Oh for the green of a lane,
Where one might lie and be lazy!
'Buzz' goes a fly in the pane;
Bluebottles drive me crazy!

Where one might lie and be lazy,
Careless of Town and all in it!—
Bluebottles drive me crazy:
I shall go mad in a minute!

Careless of Town and all in it,
With some one to soothe and to still you;—
I shall go mad in a minute;
Bluebottle, then I shall kill you!

Wish some one to soothe and to still you,
As only one's feminine kin do,—
Bluebottle, then I shall kill you:
There now! I've broken the window!

As only one's feminine kin do,—
Some muslin-clad Mabel or May!—
There now! I've broken the window!
Bluebottle's off and away!

Some muslin-clad Mabel or May,
To dash one with eau de Cologne;—
Bluebottle's off and away;
And why should I stay here alone!

To dash one with eau de Cologne,
All over one's eminent forehead;—
And why should I stay here alone!
Toiling in Town now is 'horrid.'

Haiku

A part of a syllabic verse form from thirteenth-century Japan, this unrhymed three-line poem containing 5, 7, and 5 lines respectively became popular among American poets after World War II. Originally intended as a vehicle for spiritual insight, the form under Bashō (1644–1694) embraced everyday themes with humorous intent. The following example is my own creation:

Static Cling

Fresh scent of laundry
white sheets billow from dryer
odd black sock sneaks out